627 Olson
Building the Hoover Dam

ENGINEERING MARVELS

BUILDING THE
HOOVER DAM

ELSIE OLSON

Consulting Editor, Diane Craig, M.A./Reading Specialist

Super Sandcastle

An Imprint of Abdo Publishing
abdopublishing.com

abdopublishing.com

Published by Abdo Publishing, a division of ABDO, PO Box 398166, Minneapolis, Minnesota 55439. Copyright © 2018 by Abdo Consulting Group, Inc. International copyrights reserved in all countries. No part of this book may be reproduced in any form without written permission from the publisher. Super SandCastle™ is a trademark and logo of Abdo Publishing.

Printed in the United States of America, North Mankato, Minnesota
062017
092017

THIS BOOK CONTAINS
RECYCLED MATERIALS

Editor: Rebecca Felix
Content Developer: Mighty Media, Inc.
Cover and Interior Design and Production: Mighty Media, Inc.
Photo Credits: AP Images, iStockphoto, Library of Congress, Shutterstock, Wikimedia Commons

Publisher's Cataloging-in-Publication Data

Names: Olson, Elsie, author.
Title: Building the Hoover Dam / by Elsie Olson.
Description: Minneapolis, MN : Abdo Publishing, 2018. | Series: Engineering marvels.
Identifiers: LCCN 2016962888 | ISBN 9781532111129 (lib. bdg.) | ISBN 9781680788976 (ebook)
Subjects: LCSH: Hoover Dam (Ariz. And Nev.)-- Juvenile literature. | Dams--Design and construction--Juvenile literature. | Hydraulic engineering-- Juvenile literature.
Classification: DDC 627--dc23
LC record available at http://lccn.loc.gov/2016962888

Super SandCastle™ books are created by a team of professional educators, reading specialists, and content developers around five essential components—phonemic awareness, phonics, vocabulary, text comprehension, and fluency—to assist young readers as they develop reading skills and strategies and increase their general knowledge. All books are written, reviewed, and leveled for guided reading, early reading intervention, and Accelerated Reader™ programs for use in shared, guided, and independent reading and writing activities to support a balanced approach to literacy instruction.

CONTENTS

WHAT IS A DAM?

Dams hold back water. They create lakes. They store water for drinking and farming. Dams also help make electricity. The Hoover Dam does all of these things. It is one of the world's most famous dams.

Dammed water helps farmers grow crops such as wheat.

THE HOOVER DAM

LOCATION: Colorado River, on the border of Arizona and Nevada

BUILDING STARTED:
July 7, 1930

BUILDING COMPLETED:
March 1, 1936

CHIEF ENGINEER:
Frank Crowe

HEIGHT: 726 feet (221 m)

LENGTH: 1,244 feet (379 m)

A WILD RIVER

In the 1800s, the US Southwest was hot and dry. The Colorado River flowed through the area. But the river's water was often too low or high. So the US government chose to build a dam on the river. This would control the water level.

It was hard to grow crops or find drinking water in the Southwest.

The dam was placed in the Black Canyon. The Black Canyon is on the border of Arizona and Nevada.

GETTING STARTED

Building the dam would be hard. So several building companies joined together. Frank Crowe was the chief engineer. He led the project. Gordon Kauffman was the dam's **architect**. He planned the dam's **design**.

About 21,000 men worked on the dam. Boulder City, Nevada, was built to house them.

Frank Crowe (right) and engineer Walker Young

FRANK CROWE

BORN: 1882, Trenholmville, Quebec, Canada

DIED: 1946, Redding, California

Frank Crowe was an engineer. He helped build several US dams before the Hoover Dam. Crowe found ways to build dams more quickly. The Hoover Dam's builders had a huge job. But Crowe was a strong leader. The project was finished early! Crowe went on to build four more dams.

MOVING A RIVER

The team was ready to begin. First it had to **divert** the Colorado River. Workers constructed four tunnels. These carried water around the dam site. Construction began on two structures called cofferdams. These would hold back water from the **canyon**. The river was diverted by November 1932.

Workers build one of four intake towers. The towers helped control the dam's water supply.

More than 1.5 million gallons (5.7 million L) of water moved through the tunnels each second.

DIGGING OUT

Now workers could build the dam. It needed to sit on **bedrock** to be watertight. So workers cleared the river bottom. Other workers removed loose rock from the **canyon** walls. They made the walls smooth.

Workers hung from the canyon walls to remove loose rock. These workers were called high scalers.

POURING CONCRETE

In 1933, workers began pouring concrete into blocks. The blocks would make up the dam wall. The workers sealed the blocks' **seams**. They worked every day for two years. The dam was then 660 feet (201 m) thick at the base. At the top it was 45 feet (14 m) thick.

Concrete was delivered to the dam from a mixing plant.

The first concrete block was poured on June 6, 1933.

THE DAM AT WORK

Workers began to close off the tunnels in 1934. The final tunnel was closed on February 1, 1935. Water began collecting behind the new dam. This became Lake Mead. The last concrete block was poured on May 29. President Franklin D. Roosevelt opened the dam on September 30. The Hoover Dam was the largest in the world! Its power plant opened the next year.

President Roosevelt (middle) views the dam from a mixing plant.

The Hoover Powerplant was once the largest power plant in the world. It captures the energy of falling water. It transforms this energy into electricity.

WATER, POWER, FUN

The Hoover Dam is still very important to the Southwest. It provides power to parts of Arizona, California, and Nevada. Tunnels move Lake Mead's water to many Southwestern cities. And more than 7 million people visit the dam itself each year!

Lake Mead is a popular place for fun. People swim, boat, and fish there.

DAMS OF THE WORLD

THREE GORGES DAM
LOCATION: Yangtze River, China
BUILT: 2006
HEIGHT: 607 feet (185 m)
LENGTH: 7,660 feet (2,335 m)
BENEFITS: power, flood control, deep-water path for boats

ASWAN HIGH DAM
LOCATION: Nile River, Egypt
BUILT: 1970
HEIGHT: 364 feet (111 m)
LENGTH: 12,562 feet (3,829 m)
BENEFITS: power, flood control, water supply, fishing lake

The Hoover Dam is just one of many awesome dams.
Check out these other cool dams!

ITAIPÚ DAM

LOCATION: Alto Paraná River, Brazil-Paraguay border

BUILT: 1982

HEIGHT: 643 feet (196 m)

LENGTH: 4.8-mile (7.7 km) series of dams

BENEFITS: power

GRAND COULEE DAM

LOCATION: Columbia River, Washington, United States

BUILT: 1941

HEIGHT: 550 feet (168 m)

LENGTH: 5,223 feet (1,592 m)

BENEFITS: power, flood control, water supply

MORE ABOUT THE HOOVER DAM

HARD HATS were invented while the Hoover Dam was built.

The Hoover Dam was named after US President **HERBERT HOOVER**.

The Hoover Dam contains enough concrete to **BUILD A ROAD** from New York City to San Francisco, California.

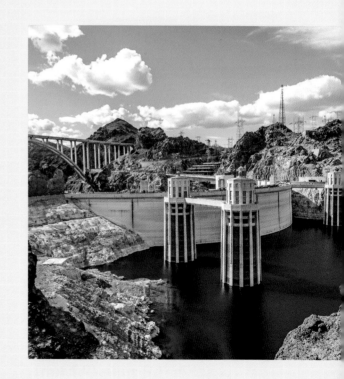

TEST YOUR KNOWLEDGE

1. On what river was the Hoover Dam built?

2. Who was the **architect** of the Hoover Dam?

3. President Herbert Hoover opened the Hoover Dam. TRUE OR FALSE?

THINK ABOUT IT!

Where does your family's drinking water and electricity come from?

ANSWERS: 1. Colorado River. 2. Gordon Kauffman. 3. False

GLOSSARY

architect - someone who designs buildings.

bedrock - the solid rock beneath soil and looser rock.

canyon - a deep, narrow river valley with steep sides.

design - the appearance or style of something.

divert - to change the course or direction in which something is moving.

seam - the line where two edges meet.